DEMOCRACY

JOHNS HOPKINS
UNIVERSITY PRESS

AARHUS UNIVERSITY PRESS

SVEND-ERIK SKAANING

DEMOCRACY

DEMOCRACY

© Svend-Erik Skaaning
and Johns Hopkins University Press 2022
Layout and cover: Camilla Jørgensen, Trefold
Cover photograph: Poul Ib Henriksen
Publishing editor: Søren Mogensen Larsen
Translated from the Danish by Heidi Flegal
Printed by Narayana Press, Denmark
Printed in Denmark 2022

ISBN 978-1-4214-4481-9 (pbk)
ISBN 978-1-4214-4480-2 (ebook)

Library of Congress Control Number: 2022930091

*Special discounts are available for bulk purchases of this
book. For more information, please contact Special Sales at
specialsales@jh.edu.*

Published in the United States by:

Johns Hopkins University Press
2715 North Charles Street
Baltimore, MD 21218-4363
www.press.jhu.edu

Published with the generous support of the
Aarhus University Research Foundation and
the Danish Arts Foundation

Purchase in Denmark: ISBN 978-87-7219-185-0

Aarhus University Press
Finlandsgade 29
8200 Aarhus N
Denmark
www.aarhusuniversitypress.dk

PEER
REVIEWED

MIX
Paper
FSC FSC® C010651

CONTENTS

DEMOCRACY-LOVERS ALL?

THE AWAKENING

As a child in Denmark in the early 1980s, I would spend election nights with my family, glued, like so many others, to the television screen as the results ticked in. The media also had daily coverage of political repression outside our comfortable little country. However, my own awareness that democracy is a hard-won right was not awakened until the summer of 1988 when, aged 10, I found myself riveted by reports of the epic events unfolding in Poland, a Communist dictatorship since World War II.

A strike that began at the shipyard in Gdansk was spreading like wildfire. Surprisingly, the Polish establishment agreed to negotiate with the opposition movement, Solidarity, whose leader – an electrician by the name of Lech Wałęsa – was elected president in 1990. Within a year of Poland's first faltering steps down the path of political reform, other Communist regimes in Central and Eastern Europe were in free fall. Today, many are Democratic members of the European Union, or EU.

These events truly opened my eyes, starting what will likely be a lifelong fascination with democracy, both as a political idea and as a form of government. Democracy remains as relevant as ever, and hopes and developments around the world raise all sorts of questions about it: What is the essence of democracy? Where and when have democracies evolved? What helps and hinders democratic development? What impacts does democracy have? And what challenges does it face today?

FROM DEGENERATE TO DARLING

The word 'democracy' comes from the Ancient Greek *demos*, 'people', and *kratos*, 'rule'. The origins of the word may be indisputable, but 'rule by the people' can mean very different things to different people. Most of us would cite freedom and equality as core element of democracy, but that brings us no closer to a definition, as the meaning of these concepts is also widely debated.

The British philosopher Walter Bryce Gallie was spot on back in 1956 when he referred to democracy as the finest example of a value-based concept with a fundamentally disputed meaning. In our day and age most people have a positive view of democracy, even though we cannot really agree on what it *is*.

Historically, 'democracy' has not always been a yes-word. In fact, not a single country we know of was governed by a democracy between the Roman Empire's conquest of the Greek city-states in 146 BCE and the revolutions in colonial America and in France, in 1776 and 1789, respectively. Democracy was largely regarded as an inferior, unsuitable form of government, and political thinkers generally remained critical, even after seeing the novel arrangements fall into place on both sides of the Atlantic.

In 1790 the father of Conservatism, an Irish-English politician named Edmund Burke, considered democracy "the most shameful thing in the world". The Danish philosopher Søren Kierkegaard was no great fan either. While the drafting of a Danish constitution was being discussed in 1848, he wrote in his journal that "Of all tyrannies, a people's government is the most excruciating, the most devoid of spirit, absolutely the downfall of all that is great and lofty."

It was only after Western democracies prevailed over Germany and her allies in *both* world wars that democracy came to be widely seen as a positive thing, and its most recent expansion took place after the Cold War ended. In 1989 the American political scientist Francis Fukuyama even said we had reached "the end of history" with liberal democracy: The only legitimate form of government was based on free and fair elections and respect for basic civil liberties.

In this light it is hardly surprising that for the vast majority of people, in Denmark and elsewhere, the word 'democracy' has positive connotations. This became clear in a global study conducted in 83 countries between 2017 and 2020. When asked whether it is good or bad to have a democratic political system, a majority of 57-98% responded it was 'good' or 'very good'.

Only a small minority of respondents rated democracy as 'very bad' or 'bad'. Countries with the lowest ratings included Iraq, Colombia, Kenya and the Philippines, while some of the highest were found in Germany, the Nordics and Zimbabwe. The ratings were 91% for China, 69% for Russia, 76% for Brazil, 88% for Indonesia, 91% for the United Kingdom, and 81% for the United States.

PUTTING ON A PRETTY HAT

The linguistic downside of 'democracy' is less pleasant. Dictators of all kinds have appropriated the word, claiming to be 'democratic' rulers. Should we laugh or cry when we learn that the North Korean constitution refers to its form of rule as a 'people's democratic dictatorship'?

Over the years, many communist or fascist regimes have tried to put a pretty hat on over their helmet, calling themselves 'people's democracies' or 'guided democracies'. Even today, some despotic rulers counter criticism by invoking a particular brand of democracy that reflects their nation's culture or serves some higher purpose.

Look at Mahathir Mohamad and Lee Kuan Yew, who for decades ruled their countries – Malaysia and Singapore – as prime ministers, but who were de facto dictators. Both claimed to have developed a special sort of democracy that placed more emphasis on 'the collective' than on individual rights, and was 'more attuned' to Asian values. Such blatant, intentional abuse of the concept of democracy is utterly meaningless.

There are many examples of misuse and abuse of this word in the public debate, where views and decisions are often denounced as 'undemocratic' by those who disagree. One may be found in an issue of the *Danish Music Journal* from 1951, which called a duty on imported gramophone records "undemocratic". More recently, Bill O'Reilly of *The O'Reilly Factor*, an American programme aired by Fox News Channel, used the same word to describe the unregulated conditions on the Internet.

In both cases controversial decisions – to introduce a duty, and not to introduce regulations – were clearly based on a democratic process, so the concept of 'democracy' was, most likely, inadvertently misconstrued. In general I suspect we should all use 'undemocratic' with greater care – unless we do not mind seeing its actual meaning watered down.

The watering can was out in Denmark in the spring of 2016 when Social Democratic leader Mette Frederiksen commented in a news broadcast on how certain imams counselled their congregations, calling it "undemocratic" that they condoned the physical punishment of children. However, despite good reasons to refuse corporal punishment, the fact that countries have not outlawed this practice, such as Denmark before 1997 and the US and many others today, does not make them undemocratic.

INHERENTLY IMPERFECT

The 2016 statement from Mette Frederiksen – Denmark's prime minister after the 2019 election – shows that many of us equate democracy with the things we like. Hitting our children is usually not in this category. Be that as it

may, a democratic process does not necessarily lead to well-reasoned decisions that we like. Direct democracy, referendums and indirect democracy via elected representatives can all result in policies that adversely affect the economy, the environment, public health, our own happiness and so forth.

In Greece, for instance, various governments spent decades pursuing irresponsible policies that nudged the country's economy towards the brink of collapse around 2010–2011. And in America nowadays it is hard to find anyone who thinks that getting involved in the Vietnam War in the early 1960s was a good idea. A rather bizarre example, also from 'the land of the free', is that democratically elected politicians have interfered in people's most private, intimate activities: In several states it remains illegal to leave the light on during intercourse, and to use sex toys or deviate from the missionary position.

Generally, it is inevitable that citizens and politicians frequently have different concerns, such as environmental sustainability and economic growth, which are not always compatible. What is more, we must acknowledge that political decisions – democratic or not – often involve *one will* prevailing over *other wills*. Invariably there are winners and losers when rules affect the redistribution of resources or give certain values priority over others. Still, rallying cries that something is 'undemocratic' hold little meaning unless the initiative directly undermines our elected representatives' ability to make political decisions.

That does not prevent us from regarding some democratically adopted policies as unjust if they do not reflect basic ideas of 'fairness and equity'. This applies to us all, regardless of our own principles or higher political ambitions – whether they are to maximize happiness, reduce the use of physical force, help the disadvantaged, seek self-actualisation or balance out arbitrary inequality. The hard truth is that justice and democracy do not always go hand in hand.

While most political philosophers see democracy as the best and only just form of rule, it is often unclear how we can adhere to detailed philosophical guidelines without forfeiting the people's right to decide policy content. A majority *can* be wrong. A majority of Germans *were* wrong when they voted for undemocratic national-socialist and communist parties in 1933, facilitating Adolf Hitler's rise to power.

ARE BRITONS REALLY SLAVES?

Fair enough, but must we agree that democracy is better than the alternatives? One obvious answer, at least initially, is found in the idea of 'collective sovereignty', fostered by the French Enlightenment philosopher Jean-Jacques Rousseau in 1762.

Rousseau believed that a political government can only be legitimate if the people make the laws. This, he says, is how to resolve the following paradox: On the one hand, laws must exist to establish and ensure freedom; on the other hand, citizens must bow to the law. The solution is that citizens themselves ensure a freedom, similar to that of 'man's natural state', by direct, collective self-determination.

As for democratic representation, it was not Rousseau's cup of tea at all, as is evident from his critique of the contemporary political system in Britain. He specifically accused the Britons of labouring under the delusion that they were free – which they only were, briefly, on election day while choosing their MPs. The next day, their enslavement resumed. No, he said, citizens ought to legislate directly.

The late 1700s nevertheless saw links forged between the democratic ideas of collective sovereignty and Republican liberal ideas of representation, division of power and civil liberties. Since that time, the core argument supporting the value of democracy per se has changed very little.

This is apparent if we follow the arguments of Robert A. Dahl, a renowned American political science professor who set out two principles: Everyone's interests must be given equal weight; and virtually all adults are competent contributors to collective decisions that concern them. These principles seem to be supported by our moral intuition, the lack of credible alternatives and our healthy scepticism of being under guardianship. If we can subscribe to these views, apparently democracy is the only legitimate form of government that exists.

DEFINING DEMOCRACY

AND THE WINNER IS ...

Democracy is all about political freedom and equity, but how do we move from this premise to an actual definition? Here, too, Professor Dahl offers help in the form of five criteria for the ideal democratic process:

First, citizens must have adequate and equal opportunities to form their preferences, to put questions on the public agenda and to express reasons for preferring one outcome over another. Second, individual citizens must be assured that their judgments will be counted as equal in weight to the judgments of others. Third, citizens must enjoy ample and equal opportunities for discovering and affirming what choice would best serve their interests. Fourth, people must have the opportunity to decide what issues are actually 'political matters', and which issues should be brought up for deliberation. Fifth and finally, political equality must extend to all adult citizens within the state or nation.

Obviously, fulfilling these criteria is very demanding. Truth be told, no existing political administration has ever done so, and most likely none ever will. There will always be inequality in individuals' resources, political ambitions and personalities, and to some degree these will undermine the ideal democratic process.

Only in a political utopia would a bank director or a professor of economics have the same political influence as an unskilled labourer or an ex-clerk on disability benefits. While each has just one vote on election day, their ability to raise agenda issues and affect politicians are vastly different. As the Norwegian political scientist Stein Rokkan once said: Votes count, but resources decide. Still, this does not make the five criteria less valuable as an ideal we can compare to our realities – a shining example of what we might achieve.

To supplement his definition of an ideal democracy, Dahl set a list of conditions that must be fulfilled in a representative democracy. First, free and frequent elections must decide who will make binding political decisions. Next, virtually all adults must have the right to vote and be eligible as candidates. Finally, citizens must have freedom of speech and the right to organise as they see fit.

Living up to these conditions is certainly more realistic than fulfilling the criteria for an ideal democratic process. Quite a few countries, including Denmark, fulfil all three conditions and have done so for many years. In fact, the quality of democracy in Denmark is so good that systematic data collected in 2021 by the Varieties of Democracy – an international research consortium also known as V-Dem – found that our small nation is the world's best when it comes to electoral and liberal aspects of democracy.

NEITHER ANGELS NOR GODS

Dahl has a term for government through free elections, with the protection of political rights and civil liberties: polyarchy, the 'rule of the many'. Critics have attacked his concept from two sides. One side, which believes we ought to make stricter demands on a democracy, includes advocates of liberal democracy, social democracy and participatory democracy. Those on the other side advocate a minimalist definition of democracy, and they are against cluttering up and mixing 'democracy as free elections and party-based competition' with all sorts of other phenomena.

After the end of World War II, these issues where hotly debated in Denmark and elsewhere. The major points presented in that discussion capture and reflect the various perspectives well. One advocate of liberal democracy at the time was a Danish law professor named Alf Ross. He wanted to expand the concept of democracy to encompass constitutionalism, including respect for a broad basket of civil liberties, checks on government and adherence to the rule of law. The aim, he said, was to safeguard individuals by stipulating limits for the government's use of force.

The contemporary philosophy professor Jørgen Jørgensen and other supporters of social democracy also emphasised the need to protect the rights of the individual, but Jørgensen reproached Ross for having a constricted view of democracy, and for not focusing on the actual inequalities in political influence. The problem, Jørgensen held, was that people's unequal tangible and intangible resources – money, education, gender, ethnicity – give them different preconditions for looking after their own interests. That is why the top priority for proponents of social democracy is achieving a more equal distribution of resources and stopping all forms of discrimination.

The Danish theology professor Hal Koch supported *both* Ross, the civil liberties advocate, *and* Jørgensen, the social equaliser, but he also emphasised that democracy is about participation and conversation. This is the fundamental premise of participatory democracy, and it is not enough to regularly give all adults *a chance to vote* in free elections. Beyond that, as many citizens as possible must actively *exercise their right to vote*.

What is more, Koch said that citizens must become involved in special-interest organisations, public rallies, parish councils, elections, demonstrations, public hearings and so forth, and they must seek to achieve political consensus. Political squabbling, he said, must be replaced by free, frank, open and reasonable consultations, which must lead, in turn, to decisions based on valid arguments rather than emotions, group affiliations or self-interest.

The Austrian economist Joseph Schumpeter could hardly have disagreed more with the supporters of participatory democracy, rejecting the very idea that democracy is an arena in which citizens, without bias, could talk their way towards the 'right' policies. He found this unrealistic, as long as people were neither angels nor gods.

Schumpeter therefore simply defines democracy as a method by which political decisions are reached, and in which citizens achieve political influence as parties compete for their votes. He does not even require an equal, universal right to vote, although there is not much *demos* in a 'democracy' where only a small minority can vote. Ultimately, minimalist democracy is found where free elections decide who holds the power to govern.

There is no doubt that all of these very different definitions of democracy share certain pivotal elements: liberty, equality, accountability and participation. But they rank and understand these elements differently, and I hardly think we will reach a consensus any time soon on who is 'right' and who is 'wrong'. What everyone ought to agree on, however, is that it is important to be open about, and aware of, what each of us perceives democracy to be. That would prevent us from wasting so much time and effort on barking up the wrong tree.

RISE, REVIVAL, RESURGENCE

ONCE UPON A TIME IN ATHENS

Most readers will know that the Ancient Greek roots
of the word 'democracy' grew from the world's first
democracies: the Greek city-states of Antiquity. The most
powerful and celebrated of these was Athens, where
democracy prevailed as early as 507 BCE.

While it is true that women, slaves and foreigners
were barred from political influence – no voting in the
legislative 'People's Assembly', and no holding office – all
male Athenians aged 20 or older were entitled to speak
and vote in the Assembly. This indisputably makes Athens,
at the very least, a minimalist democracy in Schumpeter's
sense of the word, because political decisions were made
by a sizable share of the population.

Ancient Greece had many city-states and a multitude
of constitutions. The great philosopher Aristotle collected
a total of 158, several of which were democratic.
Dēmokratía was even revered by some as a goddess, with
sacrifices and all.

Aristotle found the basic principle to be that all citizens
were to govern and be governed in turn, as the Greek
democrats wished to promote freedom, which builds on

equality. Besides upholding citizen-based political decision-making, the Athenians were intent on preventing 'career' politicians and office-holders, which would undermine the equality of political influence.

This principle is clearly reflected in the specific arrangement of their political institutions, as eminently shown by the Danish classical philologist Mogens Herman Hansen, one of the world's leading authorities on Athenian democracy.

Let us spend a moment on how Athenian democracy was organised in 355–322 BCE, the period that has been most thoroughly described. There were three key political decision-making bodies: the People's Assembly, the *nomothetai* or sworn 'legislators' and the People's Court. There was also an administration consisting of public officials, including a governing body called the Council of 500.

In the Assembly, thousands of citizens would gather to discuss political issues. The most active gave speeches, and the citizens made majority decisions by a show of hands. While the Assembly adopted temporary decrees on domestic and foreign policy, it was the job of the *nomothetai* to discuss and vote on laws that had no time limit, or were generally applicable. Their members were chosen, as needed, by the drawing of lots from a pool of 6,000 Athenians, also randomly chosen, for one year, among the citizens aged 30 or older who volunteered. This pool was additionally used as needed to select citizens for jury duty at the many People's Court sessions that dealt with all legal cases and monitored the administration.

Note that the decrees, laws and court cases were initiated by ordinary citizens. The Athenians also used lot-based rotation to appoint administrators. Among the same pool of 6,000 volunteers, 1,100 were appointed for one year, some of whom became members of the Council of 500. The Council acted as an executive committee, preparing all proposals received from the Assembly. The Council chairman was elected for one day at a time, and each citizen could only serve as a Council member twice. The administration included a further 100 citizens, 10 of them generals, all elected by the Assembly.

Generals could be re-elected, so the Athenians' legendary eagerness to draw lots did have limits. When it came to leadership in battle, they evidently gave experience some credit. What is intriguing, though, is that they were so keen to ensure citizens' political freedom and equality through direct participation – in everything from administrative matters to court decisions. Once upon a time in Athens, democracy without direct, active participation in every step of every process was all but unthinkable.

FROM SHAME TO FAME

We will smartly skip the next two millennia of world history, a long interlude in which philosophers, thinkers and political leaders put democracy in the governmental 'hall of shame'. It was only rehabilitated in the 1700s, when Enlightenment thinkers in France and Britain offered intellectual ammunition for the fight against societies based on privilege, where all power lay with the crown, the nobility and the church. But theory was one thing; practice another.

After the Declaration of Independence in 1776 and the ensuing war with Britain, 60–70% of white males in the new United States of America had the right to vote. In 1791, a constitutional amendment from 1788 guaranteed all citizens fundamental rights such as freedom of speech and assembly. Alexander Hamilton, James Madison and other Founding Fathers nevertheless chose to call their new country and its government 'a republic', because they associated 'democracy' with direct citizen's rule, as in Ancient Greece, and saw this model as neither desirable nor practically possible in a nation so large.

But views on democracy were changing. In one remarkable revival, during the French Revolution, radical Jacobites famously used the word 'democracy' as a motto on a par with "liberty, equality, fraternity", associating the concept with the election of political representatives to a parliamentary assembly. The political reforms held promise, with a liberal human rights declaration and suffrage for all tax-paying male citizens who were not servants.

The French Revolution did not lead to democracy, however, but to the Reign of Terror under Maximilien Robespierre, who sent about 17,000 alleged political opponents into the fatal embrace of Madame la Guillotine.

'Democrat' once again became an insult. Just a few staunch supporters, such as the British-American political thinker Thomas Paine and the English philosopher Jeremy Bentham, stood by democracy as an ideal.

Paine, a source of intellectual inspiration for the revolutions in France and America, basically saw democracy as a "natural right" for all human beings. By applying common sense, he said, one could ascertain the positive value of democracy. Bentham scorned this view, decrying Paine's natural rights as "nonsense upon stilts". Instead, he vehemently argued for the "utility" of democracy, convinced that it would provide the greatest happiness for the greatest number of people if citizens could look after their interests themselves, through elected representatives.

Back in America, people generally did not come to hold a positive view of democracy until the 1820s, in large part due to the founding of two political parties that vied for votes nationwide. One was the Democratic Party, led by the later president Andrew Jackson, which actively used the D-word in every political campaign.

Nothing similar happened in Europe until 1848, when a liberal, revolutionary spirit spread from France to much of Europe and Latin America. The French historian and statesman François Guizot even claimed that the word 'democracy' held such a dominant position by 1848 that all parties and governments felt obliged to use it as a slogan.

Copenhagen caught the fever too, and on 21 March

of that year citizens formed a procession that headed for Christiansborg Castle, where they petitioned Frederik VII and demanded a free constitution. The liberals in Copenhagen, as elsewhere, wanted a constitution that guaranteed civil rights, divided power into three branches – government, parliament and courts – and enabled wider political representation.

MAKE WAY FOR THE MASSES

While the ideal of democracy gained support from the mid-1800s, many still believed 'franchise' or 'suffrage' – the right to vote – ought to be limited. The vast majority found it 'unnatural' for women to have political influence, yet a few voices argued in favour of women's suffrage, notably the British philosopher John Stuart Mill.

The Irish-American writer John Boyle O'Reilly called female suffrage an "unjust, unreasonable, unspiritual abnormality". It would merely be an unnecessary burden that women were ill-equipped to handle. Today few call voting rights for women into doubt, but back in their day the 'suffragettes' and their sympathisers fought long and hard around the world. New Zealand was the first country to allow all adult citizens to vote, but not until 1893.

In addition, the upper classes in many countries were averse to voting rights for people without a certain amount of property, income or schooling. They mainly feared that the poor, ignorant masses would elect narrow-minded, inept representatives and use their political power to redistribute resources and undermine public morals.

Denmark got her Constitution in 1849, a document which, for its time, extended suffrage quite broadly, although it excluded seven specific groups still known as 'the Seven F's', which were: 'footmen, felons, fortuneless, failures, females, foreigners and fools'. To modern Danes, the original 'F-words' are similarly odd and archaic, although not vulgar, and here is what they mean: servants with no household of their own, convicted citizens, recipients of poverty support, bankrupt citizens, women, foreign citizens and insane people under guardianship. Today, only the last two categories remain excluded from voting in national elections.

The F-limitations left roughly two thirds of adult Danes disenfranchised, but even this did not satisfy J.B.S. Estrup, a prominent landowner and head of government. He called the new, broader suffrage in Denmark "the most dim-witted of schemes" at a time when there was "certainly no shortage of idiotic suggestions".

The revolutionary Jacobites had already included suffrage for all adult males in the French Constitution of 1793 – but France held no elections while it was in force, making Liberia and Greece the first to introduce general male suffrage, in 1839 and 1844, respectively. France and Switzerland followed in 1848 but were quite late in giving suffrage to women, in 1944 and 1971, respectively.

Various voting criteria illustrate how ingeniously the elite sought to limit political influence to select groups in the 1800s and early 1900s. In the Netherlands, for instance, adult men could only vote if they could prove they paid over a certain amount in direct taxes or in rent, or owned a household. Alternatively, they could earn a minimum annual wage, hold a certain amount in bank deposits or national bonds, or have a certificate or degree in certain professions. The strangest qualification may have been owning or renting a vessel with a freight capacity of 24 tonnes or more.

Latin American elites initially limited voting in less concrete ways. In many cases, local election authorities could grant a man the right to vote or stand for election if he was a *vecino*, a 'neighbour'. Figuratively this meant he was a recognised member of the local community, most often with a respected profession and ample funds to cover his daily needs.

We find another solution to the 'problem' of keeping political influence beyond the reach of the unendowed in Belgium, effective in 1893–1919, when well-educated and wealthy Belgian men could cast three votes. Men who possessed just one of these qualities had two votes, and the rest – the poor and uneducated – had just one vote.

Prussia ensured voting inequality in another way. The realm's most wealthy people, typically landowners, who paid one third of the country's direct taxes, were collectively allotted one third of the vote. The much larger group of men with middling incomes, who also paid about one third of taxes, also got about a third. Finally, the impoverished majority, about 85% of the population, which paid the last third of direct taxes, had to make do with one third of the votes. This clever system gave the wealthiest 15% of citizens twice as many votes as all the rest combined.

After the American Civil War of 1861–1865 between North and South, barring people from voting because of race, creed or colour was made illegal, but in practice discrimination continued. In some states, potential voters had to prove they could read and speak English, but the white officials who tested and registered prospective voters were often prejudiced, failing even highly educated black people while passing white people whose test results were less than mediocre.

There were also many impoverished white men in the South who could invoke the 'grandfather clause', giving them the right to vote if their grandfather had been qualified to vote before the Civil War, or had served in the military. This applied to just a tiny fraction of black men's grandfathers.

Today, around the world, most formal restrictions on voting eligibility have been lifted. In Denmark, 'females' and 'footmen' were permitted to vote in 1915. Most remaining restrictions apply to very small groups, such as military personnel in Kuwait and Brazil, monks in Thailand and Myanmar, and felons in certain American states. At present, only Brunei and Saudi Arabia have not formally granted their citizens the right to vote in national elections.

FIDDLING AND FIXING

There are many other ways to curtail political opposition.

After most of Latin America became independent between 1808 and 1826, its regimes and rulers have routinely used ballot fraud and other corrupt methods to remain in power.

One contemporary observer of the Colombian elections in 1898 remarked that all was made ready for the final scene of an election farce. Contending with the government's fiddling and fixing, the opposition was destined to fail, and the few candidates who won a seat in parliament were merely meant to lend some legitimacy to the charade.

Things were little better in Argentina. At the elections in 1876 and 1886, government troops surrounded polling stations to prevent opposition supporters from voting. The ruling party also bought votes, bribed sworn officials and destroyed votes cast for rival candidates, and names of opposition-friendly voters were mysteriously struck from electoral rolls while names of government-friendly voters – often newly arrived immigrants not even eligible to vote – would suddenly appear.

If these methods fell short of the desired result, regimes had no problem cancelling the election. Even in a country like Costa Rica, a democratic darling in the region, election scholars have found 47 different types of election fixing that occurred in the early 1900s.

Until the 1960s a good deal of election fraud also went on in the US, especially at a local level. The political life of certain cities, not least Chicago, was inextricably linked to organised crime, with close ties between politicians and the Mafia. In the South, the Democratic Party used illegal methods to maintain power after the Civil War. The Ku Klux Klan and other white supremacist groups even used threats and violence to prevent black citizens from voting, and to keep their opponents from gaining a political foothold. One infamous election in North Carolina in 1876 resulted in some 150 black lives being lost. A vastly larger number were victims of financial pressure and terror: Do as you are told or you will lose your job, see your house burned down or end up dangling from a tree.

The European continent also had its fair share of election fraud. The Soviet Union almost routinely published official elections results that showed 99.9% of votes going to the ruling Communist Party. As the Soviet dictator Joseph Stalin reportedly said: "I consider it completely unimportant who [...] will vote, or how; but what is extraordinarily important is this – who will count the votes, and how."

Prior to World War I, it was common practice in Spain, Romania and Bulgaria for the king to appoint a new prime minister when an existing government had made a blunder or was getting stale. The new prime minister would then declare a pro forma election and swindle his way to a comfortable parliamentary majority, feeding ballot boxes with fake votes and preventing opposition supporters from voting at all.

Cunning manipulation of elections included keeping voters away by locating polling stations for opposition-friendly neighbourhoods in inappropriate places – like a hospital ward full of contagion – or having individuals vote multiple times, occasionally on behalf of dead or fictitious people or political opponents. Sometime there was even an announcement, during vote-counting, that an opposition candidate had withdrawn – even though they had not.

Denmark, Norway, Sweden and Germany were less affected by fraudulent election practices. However, the fact remains that in these countries the government was appointed by the king and *not* by the elected parliament. Parliamentary democracy was not introduced in Denmark until 1901, after which time the government could not remain in power if there was a parliamentary majority against it in the Folketing.

This new practice remained disputed until the ultimate stress test in 'the Easter Crisis' of 1920, when Christian X – spurred on by the Liberal Party and the Conservative People's Party – dismissed the incumbent Social Liberal prime minister C.T. Zahle. This went directly against the Folketing majority, which consisted of the Social Liberals and Social Democrats. After massive demonstrations and threats of a general strike, the king backed down, and all parties agreed that it was time for an election.

Nowadays a small and ever-dwindling minority of countries have governments that are actually responsible to a monarch rather than to a parliamentary assembly. These are largely limited to the Arab world, notably Jordan, Kuwait and Morocco.

On the other hand, in many countries, particularly in

Africa and Asia, various forms of manipulation continue to undermine formal democratic elections. The 2013 general election in Zimbabwe is a good example. The incumbent president, Robert Mugabe, ensured re-election for himself and his associates through strongly biased media coverage, and by installing his supporters in the electoral commission, the courts and the police. This was a practical way of affecting voter registration and the casting and counting of ballots.

Regrettable scenarios of this sort are no surprise for those who trust Lord Acton, the British historian who famously observed that power corrupts, and absolute power corrupts absolutely. Others use an aphorism that puts a witty twist on a grim reality, saying that politicians, like diapers, should be changed often, and for the same reasons.

FOR MY FRIENDS, EVERYTHING; FOR MY ENEMIES, THE LAW

Another type of political repression is also declining globally: the banning of political organisations. Many of the socialist parties and labour unions emerging in the latter 1800s were suppressed, and right-wing military dictatorships were, and are, generally the worst oppressors.

Even the Danish socialists had a rocky start. On 5 May 1872, police and military forces were used to dissolve the peaceful workers' demonstration taking place at the Northern Common in Copenhagen. 'The Battle on the

Common' was followed by a ban on the Danish chapter of the Internationale – the precursor of the country's Social Democratic Party. Communist regimes have been equally repressive of centrist–liberal movements and all other elements that typify independent civil societies.

In the nineteenth century, conservative elites opposed freedom of speech as strongly as they did universal suffrage, fearing it would cause unrest by spreading lies and wickedness, or even seduce the masses into thinking they were competent to play a part in ruling the nation. Basically, those in power were afraid of criticism and organised opposition.

Consider the French general Napoleon Bonaparte, who usurped power in 1799 in the tumultuous void after the revolution. Declaring himself Emperor five years later, he remarked that it would be impossible to remain in power for even three months if he allowed a free press.

At the end of the Napoleonic wars in 1815, only Norway and the United States could honestly say they had any sort of free press. By the mid-1800s the governments in the Benelux countries, the Scandinavian countries and Britain had ended censorship, whereas Bulgaria, Austria-Hungary and Germany had severe press restrictions until after World War I, despite formally ending censorship years earlier.

A Czech historian complained in 1830 that one's range of topics was largely limited to cookbooks, prayer books and fairy tales, and a French journalist declared in 1841 that if everything readers knew about Germany came from their newspapers, they "would have come to the conclusion that German life consisted of hunting and eating."

Today it is rare to see actual bans on opposition parties. However, one does see more sophisticated forms of deceit, including manipulation of candidate eligibility rules and election donations, the abuse of tax and libel law, and biased media coverage.

The list of journalists killed since 1992 numbers more than 1449 cases worldwide. The vast majority of victims wrote about politics, war, human rights and corruption. Major contributors to this appalling statistic are Iraq, the Philippines, Algeria, Colombia, Russia and Pakistan – which also rank predictably low in general surveys of press freedom. Countries that flunk this discipline include Eritrea, North Korea, China, Turkmenistan and Syria, while the aces are primarily wealthy Western countries, with the Nordics at the top.

GIANT LEAPS, WITH OCCASIONAL STANDSTILLS AND SETBACKS

In various parts of the world the introduction of democracy has been fraught with problems, although great progress has been made over the past 200 years, as I touched on earlier. Now, let us first look at the number of minimalist democracies where the power to govern is actually decided in competitive elections.

Since 1900 the number of democracies has risen from 10 to about 125, or roughly two thirds of the world's nations. In the early 1800s, the only countries fulfilling the criteria for minimalist democracy were the United States and, rather later, Belgium and Britain, in 1830 and 1832, respectively.

The liberal revolution in the Western world around 1848 saw democracy flourish in Switzerland, France and elsewhere, although reactionary movements often made successful countermoves, so it was only after World War I that small, gradual increments became an upsurge.

In 1920 almost all European countries were ruled by popularly elected governments, but many new democracies soon failed. In fact, the interwar period is the only time in modern history that saw a significant loss of democracy. The Italian dictator Benito Mussolini's fascist March on Rome in 1922 was an early sign of democratic decline. Several similar takeovers followed, including the National Socialist Party's rise to power in Germany in 1933, and General Franco's coup in Spain in 1936.

But the end of World War II gave democracy new momentum in many countries recently freed from occupation by Germany, Italy and Japan – which also returned to democracy themselves. After this, the relatively stable number of minimalist democracies persisted from the 1950s to the late 1970s, when it gradually began to grow.

The fall of the Berlin Wall in 1989 was a clarion call, and the end of the Cold War saw a veritable floodtide of democracy sweep across the world. But the wave soon petered out, and since the mid-1990s the total number of democracies has changed very little.

Obviously this does not mean that all remaining dictatorships are stable and will never be succeeded by democracies, or vice versa. The general trends cover a large number of regime changes in individual countries. Argentina, for instance, went through no less than five transitions to democracy and four collapses of democracy between 1911 and 1983. In Thailand, the nation's fourth transition to democracy, in 2011, fell apart just three years later after yet another military coup.

All told, from 1788 to 2020 there have been some 269 transitions to democracy, and about 145 democratic breakdowns. Since 2005, transitions and collapses have largely broken even, looking strictly at the numbers.

Today the old democracies in Western Europe, North America, Australia and New Zealand have been joined by numerous democracies in Eastern Europe, Latin America, sub-Saharan Africa and South and East Asia. However, dictatorships still exist in all the regions in the latter group, where countries continue to enter and leave the democratic camp. In Central Asia and the Arab world democracy has not gained ground, with Mongolia as a remarkable exception.

WHAT MAKES DEMOCRACY BLOOM?

EXPLANATIONS APLENTY

Faced with so many transitions to and from democracy, a scholar instinctively searches for patterns and reasons. Long ago, Aristotle described two situations in which democracy would plausibly arise: after suppression and mass uprising; or after a split in the ruling elite, one faction joining with the masses.

Much later, in the 1500s, the political thinker Niccolò Machiavelli of Florence emphasised that for democracy to grow, citizens must be equal and virtuous. Rousseau later agreed, adding that a country must be small and have a culturally homogeneous population.

Thinkers and scholars have since proposed countless factors that they believe help or hamper democracy. In my own PhD work I resolved to count all the factors mentioned in academic studies. I reached a total of 42 and have since come across several more.

In the following I deal with three clusters of explanations that go a bit deeper than many surface-scraping accounts of historic figures – although great figures like Nelson Mandela of South Africa and

Václav Havel of Czechoslovakia have played epic roles in fostering democracy. Both had moderate, pensive personalities, overwhelming popular support and similar political paths, starting out as members, then leaders of important opposition movements and ending up as elected presidents.

THE PARADOX OF PLENTY

A look around the globe after World War II soon reveals that rich countries have tended to be democracies, while poor countries are overrepresented among its dictatorships. A comparison between Western Europe and sub-Saharan Africa shows the difference: The former, with certain exceptions in Southern Europe, has typically had stable democracies, whereas the latter has been dominated by party-based or military dictatorships. This has motivated social scientists to investigate the underlying mechanisms and links.

Many researchers stress that transitioning from an agrarian society to an industrial or service-based economy strengthens the middle class and the working class, to the detriment of the landed nobility, which historically had a firm grip on power. The underlying logic is that economic development often helps equalise the power resources in a society, as education levels generally rise while income inequalities fall.

One effect is that the social groups with the greatest interest in civil liberties and universal suffrage become stronger in their struggle against reactionary forces. But greater resource equality also means that a tiny elite has less to lose by giving democratic concessions to the masses, because a broader tax base reduces the risk of the elite's assets and incomes being heavily taxed.

Other researchers suggest that economic development leads to a shift in the population's values: With more resources available to them, people shift their focus away from procuring basic necessities like food, clothing and shelter. Instead, they begin to wish more for self-actualisation and active participation in civil society, which is more in tune with the boons of democracy than with the burdens of dictatorship.

While all these mechanisms typically make wealthy countries democratic, there are exceptions. Obvious examples are the oil-producing nations in the Middle East, such as Kuwait, Bahrain and Saudi Arabia. All three have an extremely high gross domestic product (GDP) per capita, but none are remotely similar to a textbook democracy. There is a good reason for this: Oil and, to a lesser degree, other natural resources do not increase but *reduce* the potential for democracy to bloom. This is known as 'the resource curse', or 'the paradox of plenty'.

For one thing, such countries have not lived and worked their way through an industrialisation process which, through social partners constantly bickering and bargaining, gradually shifts power – so apparently, money must be 'hard-earned' to promote democracy. Another thing is that 'easy money' from oil is often used to safeguard those in power, with security services that come down hard on the opposition. Thirdly, oil money enables governments to 'bribe' the population with public positions and social benefits and services – without needing taxes to finance these amenities.

Very broadly speaking, economic development tends to affect the stability of democracies rather than their genesis and emergence. That makes it hard to identify a particular level of development at which countries achieve democratic transition. But if a country has become democratic, for whatever reason, then compared to a poor country, a rich country is far more likely to remain democratic, as we see historically in interwar Europe.

Soon after World War I, virtually all European countries became democratic. By the outbreak of World War II, however, the region had a 'rotten banana' of failed democracies, stretching from Southern Europe across the Balkan, over Eastern and Central Europe right up to the Baltic countries in the north-east. With these areas being Europe's least economically and socially developed, the democracies there were not very resilient.

Reactionary right-wing forces took power in one country after another, often boosted by the winds of crisis blowing across the continent. It is true that Germany, Austria and the northern regions of Italy, where fascism was strongest, were relatively well developed and had strong civil societies, but their populations were disappointed with the results of World War I, and there was such a lack of will to collaborate across the political spectrum that their democracies broke down as well.

PRIVILEGED PROTESTANTS?

In the early 1900s, the German sociologist Max Weber emphasised that culture shapes our views and behaviours, thereby shaping democratic and economic development. In keeping with Weber's thinking, the interwar years showed a conspicuous overlap between Protestant majority populations on the one hand, and affluence and surviving democracies on the other. In fact, all independent Protestant countries were stable democracies throughout the interwar period, whereas most Catholic countries and all Greek Orthodox countries went through democratic collapse – if they had been democracies at all.

The renowned political scientist Samuel P. Huntington believed that Protestantism supports democracy because it emphasises personal freedom, separates politics and religion, promotes education of the masses and active participation in society, and supports the rule of law. Conversely, Huntington says, Greek Orthodox, Confucian and Muslim faiths and cultures hinder democracy because they emphasise collectivism over individualism. On Islam, in particular, some have noted that it is a prescriptive religion that leaves too little elbow room for democratic policies.

Many have challenged the suggestion that religion and democracy are linked. Sceptics point out that, generally, almost all religions and cultures have some elements that pull towards democracy and others that push against it. What is more, religions and cultures are not static but in constant flux, as the following examples show.

If we look at Martin Luther's own writings from the 1500s, which expressed the core elements of Protestant thought, they contain no direct support of democracy, to put it mildly. Contrariwise, a declaration from the Catholic Church, following one session of the Second Ecumenical Council of the Vatican in 1962–1965, supported the idea of democracy as the preferred form of rule.

Traditionally, the Pope and his proselytes had supported reactionary forces in fighting church-critical liberals and socialists. The shift of the Holy See proved to be crucial, particularly in Latin America and Poland, where the Catholic Church offered a free space of sorts where criticism could be voiced. Today most Catholic and Greek Orthodox countries are democratic, as are a number of countries – Mongolia, India, Japan and Senegal, for example – where most people are *not* professing Christians.

Finally, the Protestant denominations and their adherents were not always inclined to democracy. After the Reformation in the 1500s, in which several European counties embraced Protestantism, the kings practised absolute rule 'by the grace of God' and with the support of the church. Much later, in interwar Germany, the Nazis had more supporters among Protestants than among Catholics. And during Colonialism, white Protestants in developing countries were reluctant to share their democratic rights with the colonised populations. It was the non-violent struggle against this particular brand of discrimination in South Africa and India that earned Mahatma Gandhi world renown.

The example of Gandhi evokes the issue of ethnic, linguistic and religious diversity, something John Stuart Mill, whom we met earlier, saw as a potential stumbling block for democracy: A variety of cultures can nurture sharp distinctions between 'us' and 'them'. What is more, political disputes about cultural issues are often important enough to quell citizens' desire to compromise. According to the prominent social scientist Robert Putnam, the blooming of democracy is unlikely in places with strong bonding *within* certain groups but little bridging *across* groups.

The many ethnic and religious conflicts in Iraq, Georgia, Nigeria and other struggling nations paint a dismal picture for democracy's future in countries with great cultural diversity. Generally, however, there is no strong link between ethnic or religious diversity per se and the risk of violent conflict. The UK, Switzerland, the Netherlands, Indonesia, Ghana and, to some extent, India show that peaceful democratic coexistence despite large differences is possible. Serious problems chiefly arise when different groups have less political influence than their size merits or see their basic rights suppressed by the government.

Even in more homogeneous countries, democracy is not guaranteed. A political culture where the elite and the masses specifically support democratic rights does not grow and bloom on its own. Fortunately, citizens in democracies tend, gradually, to become quite fond of democracy – or if not, then unable to see a more desirable alternative. Today, Denmark and other established democracies have hardly anyone who opposes democracy. All major parties represented in the Folketing openly support free elections and civil rights, and very few are active in movements that directly oppose democracy.

STICKS AND CARROTS

Obviously, democracy cannot thrive in a country whose population no longer controls its own destiny, as when Denmark was occupied by Germany in World War II. It is equally obvious that the Allied forces, and the US in particular, played a decisive role in reintroducing democratic governments in Germany, Japan and Italy after World War II.

International influence can also be more indirect. After the 1974 collapse of the authoritarian regime in Portugal with the Carnation Revolution and its diplomatic aftermath, similar things were soon happening in Spain, and in both countries' former colonies in Latin America – a sort of democratic domino effect.

An even clearer cross-border knock-on effect was seen after the popular uprising in Poland in 1989, sweeping across Hungary, Czechoslovakia, Bulgaria, Romania and the Baltics. In a much later example, further south, the world watched in wonderment as the Tunisians ousted the dictator Ben Ali in 2011, awakening pro-democratic protest among Egyptians, Libyans, Yemenites and Syrians.

Clearly, populations and ruling elites take inspiration from developments in other countries, especially if they have a shared history, language or religion, but whether popular revolutions lead to viable democracies is quite a different matter. After the surge of democratic sentiments in North Africa, known as the 'Arab Spring', disappointed observers are now talking about an 'Arab Winter' dominated by civil wars and new autocratic governments.

Especially after World War II, many Western democracies have tried to cultivate the resurgence of democracy. Seeking to promote democracy abroad, they have introduced trade sanctions, notified aid recipients of democratic reform requirements, and supported civil rights groups, political parties and elections.

Unfortunately, in many cases such efforts have not borne fruit. While sub-Saharan Africa has hardly any remaining dictatorships that do not hold elections and allow opposition candidates, countries like Rwanda and Uganda still have huge problems with the quality of their elections.

The prospects of ending up with a viable democracy are not good if the country's elite does not play along, and if the pro-democracy voices and civil society are not strong enough to keep the rulers in check. In such conditions, the population, and the donors, are all too often fobbed off with a government that resembles a democracy on the surface but is actually an oligarchy – a 'rule of the few'.

There is strong evidence that the sticks and carrots

wielded by rich democracies only really make a difference if there are strong economic, security-related and social ties upholding them. This means that effective support for democracy depends on geographical proximity and shared elements of culture and history. The best example of this is, perhaps, the positive influence from older EU countries on former Communist countries in the eastern region of Central Europe, where Western democracies initially served as examples worth emulating.

The ties between countries were later reinforced when trade grew explosively, NATO was expanded, and citizens and politicians began to travel around Europe as never before. This influence became more active and intentional as EU leaders began to tempt former East Bloc countries with EU accession if certain terms, 'the Copenhagen Criteria', were fulfilled. These include having a market economy, free competition and a liberal, democratic government.

An example that illustrates the limits of external democracy support is the 2007 general election in Kenya. Never before had Western donors invested so massively in conducting free and fair elections in Africa. Good intentions notwithstanding, the country ended up on the brink of a civil war among different ethnic groups. And recent developments in Afghanistan and Iraq, following the external removal of the Taleban and Saddam Hussein, highlight the difficulties of implanting a robust democracy from the outside, rather than nurturing home-grown, grassroots initiatives.

BUT DOES IT MAKE A DIFFERENCE?

HOLD YOUR HORSES

The end of the Cold War was followed by a period of euphoric optimism among democracy devotees, but Huntington sought to calm the democratic equestrians by underscoring that democracy, by definition, solves the problem of tyranny, but – alas! – cannot necessarily solve many other problems in the world. At the end of the day you cannot eat voting rights or seek shelter under a free constitution. Achieving universal suffrage is one thing; improving living standards quite another.

In this light, the American president Abraham Lincoln did not quite clear the fence on his own democratic thoroughbred when he said, during the Civil War, that democracy was a government "of the people, by the people, for the people". The problem is the third and highest bar in his definition, which implies that democratic decisions must be in the people's best interest, and as noted earlier, democracy does not always mean sound decision-making.

Two out of three ain't bad. But does it really make a difference? Or does democracy generally have a poorer track record than dictatorships in delivering wealth, well-being, liberty and security?

CHINESE DRAGON VS INDIAN ELEPHANT

Many people intuitively assume that there is a positive link between democracy and prosperity. First of all, populations generally want economic and social progress, which politicians in a democracy feel pressured to promote – or wave goodbye to re-election.

Dictators, not being accountable, can more easily feather their own nest. This ties in with the second factor: the civil liberties in a democracy. Free speech, in particular, inhibits corruption and helps the government and companies to make better-informed decisions about which policies and investments are worth pursuing.

But comparing China and India, the world's most populous nations, this is not what we see. India has been a democracy since throwing off British colonial rule in 1947. Meanwhile, China has been under Communist rule since 1949. One might readily presume that India would be in the better position today, especially because China was slightly less developed in the late 1940s.

However, the plain numbers for 2020 from the United Nations' development organisation, UNDP, paint a different picture. For instance, in China, schooling on average lasts 8.1 years, but the figure is only 6.5 years in India. Or take average life expectancy, which differs by eight years: 77 years in China, but 70 in India. China is also best on economic growth, with a per capita GNI around

16,057 US dollars, compared with 6,681 dollars for India. The dragon seems to be outperforming the elephant. So perhaps a firm-handed dictatorship is preferable after all, and capable of marshalling an entire nation's energy to push in one direction?

Or perhaps it is not, considering the Danish UNDP numbers for 2020: an average 12.6 years of education, a life expectancy of 81 years and a per capita GNI around 58,662 dollars. The comparable numbers for the US are 13.4 years of education, a life expectancy of 79 years and a per capita GNI of 63,826 dollars. So although China is ahead of India, these metrics put China well behind developed Western countries. Bear in mind also that the Chinese equation includes various ideologically motivated horrors. The first was the Great Leap Forward (1958–1961), when forced industrialisation and collectivisation led to severe famine. Later came the Cultural Revolution (1966–1976), with extensive physical and mental repression and brutality.

You might think the sombre lesson from China is that people may have to relinquish basic rights to achieve progress. As Vladimir Lenin, the Communist leader of the Russian Revolution in 1917, cynically remarked: If you want to make an omelette, you have to break some eggs.

For democracy defender now ready to trade their kingdom for a horse, here comes some good news: Denmark and other countries, not least the Nordics, show it is possible to achieve positive development without extreme oppression. A high-level comparison of whether democracy or dictatorship serves the general population best gives us further cause for optimism, although not outright euphoria.

Newly introduced democracy cannot be expected to have much impact from one year to the next, but dictatorships seem no better at ensuring economic growth and public welfare. While China has markedly improved living standards for all, there are numerous examples of undemocratic countries that are doing very poorly on that parameter, pushing the comparison in the opposite direction. Unfortunately, there is an extremely long list of dictators who have exploited power to enrich themselves and their friends and relatives.

One notable example is the Congolese ruler Mobutu Sese Seko, whose wine cellars reputedly held over 15,000 exclusive bottles, and who spent millions to fly in fresh foods, hairdressers and stylists from around the world. Another is the Libyan colonel and ruler Muammer Gaddafi, who reportedly died the world's richest man, with a fortune of some 200 million dollars.

Others paragons of excess are Ferdinand Marcos of the Philippines, whose wife, as they fled, left behind more than 800 handbags and 1,000 pairs of shoes; the Haitian ruler 'Baby Doc' Duvalier, whose impoverished country paid for his two-million-dollar wedding; Saddam Hussein of Iraq, who built 70 luxury palaces for his personal use; and Robert Mugabe, who, before relinquishing power in Zimbabwe at age 93, reportedly spent around 15 million dollars on luxury trips with his wife – in six months.

Outside this new 'hall of shame', findings from several new studies suggest that, all in all, democracy has a positive impact: The *more democratic* a country has been, and the *longer* it has been a democracy, the better it performs. In other words, there is little use in being an imperfect democracy for just a few years, as many interwar democracies were.

In contrast, a country that holds free elections and promotes civil liberties for a long period of time can expect things to get better. And, rather predictably, things look even brighter if a country's politicians have a reliable and efficient public administration to carry out their decisions, observing rules and regulations. Once again the Nordic countries are good examples.

LET THE KILLING BEGIN

This research may be sound, but as the French political thinker Alexis de Tocqueville shrewdly noted back in the mid-1800s, democracy has an inherent risk of developing into a 'tyranny of the majority'. Under such rule, he hypothesised, society is minutely regulated, leaving no room for original thought or creative activities. The preoccupation with equality is so pervasive that the masses prefer a state of enslaved equality rather than inequality in an otherwise free society.

Luckily, in the real world, countries that hold fair elections and abide by the outcomes usually also systematically permit critical statements and associations. Once again, by definition a true democracy will uphold freedom of expression, assembly and organisation, given that these are all democratic rights.

Democracy also does better than dictatorships on freedom of religion and free movement, and on the right to own property. It is highly unusual for public authorities in democracies to persecute, say, atheists or practitioners of a certain religion.

The situation is very different in many dictatorships. In North Korea, citizens caught with a Bible are tortured and risk death. In Saudi Arabia, where a particular version of sharia, Islamic canonical law, is a central pillar of society, apostasy – leaving the religion – carries the death penalty, and only Muslims of the Sunni persuasion are allowed to practise their religion in public.

Furthermore, democracies rarely limit or prohibit citizens from travelling inside or outside their country, whereas military dictatorships in Latin America and Asia have often exiled leading opposition leaders, refusing them re-entry or putting them under house arrest. Communist countries had laborious processes for getting a permit to travel abroad, and countries like Albania granted just a handful each year during the Cold War. Citizens also needed an official permit to move house or take an extended holiday in their own country.

Finally, dictatorial systems offer numerous examples of companies and country homes being confiscated without compensation to the owner. This is logical, as dictatorial power typically relies on support from a small elite, which can be pampered with property taken from others.

This is a no-go strategy in a democracy, where private ownership is widely protected and respected by the population, and by the balanced powers of the government, parliament and courts. Naturally, this is something domestic and foreign investors appreciate.

But what about security and peace? Scholars have found a very strong link between democracy and the absence of murder, torture and other state-sanctioned oppression. In democracies, the police and armed forces rarely commit politically motivated violence, which is all too common under non-democratic regimes.

If we look in isolation at three Communist regimes – Joseph Stalin's in the USSR, Mao Zedong's in China and Pol Pot's in Cambodia – they purportedly caused 21–70 million deaths. The killing in Cambodia wiped out about one fourth to one third of the entire population.

Most people are painfully aware of the many atrocities, not least the Holocaust, committed by the Nazis under the leadership of Adolf Hitler. Another less known dictator was Idi Amin, who ruled Uganda in 1971–1979. He had his own combined holiday home and torture centre on the small island of Mukusu in Lake Victoria. Here, Amin would subject political opponents to unspeakable torments, including dismemberment and genital mutilation, before feeding them to the crocodiles.

Abandoning this grisly image to focus instead on peace among nations, Tocqueville believed that citizens in a democracy have a great capacity for compassion. However, they are also less apt to give in to passionate emotions. He believed these features, taken together, were a poor basis for a militaristic mentality, lessening democrats' inclination to go to war. Even so, scholars find little to support any claim that democracies go to war less often than dictatorships. This is clear from the relatively numerous violent interventions conducted or assisted by democracies after the Cold War in the theatres of former Yugoslavia, Afghanistan, Iraq, Mali, Libya and Syria.

On the other hand, various research findings support what has become known as 'the democratic peace hypothesis': Democracies do not make war on each other. Early on, in 1795, the German Enlightenment philosopher Immanuel Kant pointed out that while it is easy for a dictator to declare war, the citizens of a democracy are more hesitant – knowing they will have to bear all the burdens of it.

Furthermore, democracies have a set of shared values that put a lid on mutual aggression. And the hypothesis seems to hold true. Actually, there is no good example of a war fought by two or more modern democracies. That is why my colleagues and I often emphasise the democratic peace hypothesis as the closest thing we get to an empirical law in the social sciences.

I wrote "modern democracies" because the theory clearly did not apply to the city-states of ancient Greece. Looking at the writings of Herodotus and Thucydides, recognised as the fathers of historical method, we find accounts of citizens gathered at a people's assembly and eagerly voting in favour of war, knowing full well they would have to fight in the front line themselves.

Inspired by the hypothesis of democratic peace among nations, some suggest that democracy also prevents the outbreak of civil strife. They argue that citizens in democracies are more satisfied, due to the freedom and influence they enjoy. What is more, democratic elections are a legitimate, non-violent way of handling political disputes, as also noted by the Austrian philosopher Karl Popper. Lastly, there is usually little support for deciding disputes through violent conflict because the costs, just as in international conflicts, will ultimately fall back on the citizens.

Other studies stress that dictatorships usually remain as peaceful as democracies, mainly because dictators are prepared to ruthlessly quash any insurgence. Generally, the greatest risk of civil war is found under hybrid regimes, as in Rwanda and Uganda. These typically have an intermediate level of political freedom and repression, with room for the growth of political opposition groups but little or no room for them to gain power.

Regrettably, it is hard to form a clear picture of which arguments carry most weight. Different scholars and analysts arrive at different results, but it is reasonable to conclude that, overall, a high level of democracy coincides with the lowest risk of civil war.

DEMOCRACY IN DANGER?

SOUNDING THE ALARM

There is much focus on whether democracies perform better than non-democratic alternatives, and rightly so. If they seem not to, there will be dissatisfaction all around, among elites as well as ordinary citizens. This can be a particular threat to the world's young democracies.

Pessimists in old democracies in North America and Western Europe also lament democracy's decline, with a loss of quality in its institutions and processes, but these are new lyrics set to an old tune that echoes back even to ancient Greece and the writings of Plato and Aristotle.

Few modern pessimists envision Western countries suddenly, violently, becoming repressive dictatorships. They are more worried about a subtle, gradual undermining of political and civil liberties and equality, an issue high on their agenda. Politically, the doomsayers of democracy inhabit both left and right in the party landscape, but the two camps often highlight different problems.

First, there is the tension between collective security and civil liberties. Too often the world has seen this tension brutally unleashed – with episodes in recent years at clubs in Paris, the airport in Brussels, Utøya island west of Oslo, hotels in Tunisia, a church in Charleston, SC, villages across Nigeria and even London Bridge.

Demands for more surveillance and control are countered by warnings that stricter measures will go too far and undermine our democratic rights.

This problem is not as new as it may seem. Democracies have always faced the dilemma of whether they should tolerate intolerance, and if so, how much. If we look to the wording of the Danish Constitution, it allows the prohibition of societies and associations that incite or encourage violence. Even so, in the spring of 2016 the Liberal prime minister at the time, Lars Løkke Rasmussen, asserted that the Constitution ought to be challenged and its limits for political action tested. His statements were prompted by disquieting hate speech from Muslim clerics in Denmark, and by the rise of 'parallel communities' in what is generally a very homogeneous society. While a democracy must have the right to defend itself, there is good reason to consider restrictions carefully.

Many constraints affect not only enemies of democracy but ordinary citizens as well. We regularly hear stories of 'stop-and-frisk zones' or monitoring of personal communication by public authorities like the US National Security Agency, or private companies like Google and Facebook. Then there is the self-censorship, induced by our fear of terrorist wrath, which makes us tread carefully when exercising our freedom of speech and expression. Today, who would dare to draw, let alone publish, a cartoon of the Prophet Mohammed – especially in France, after the horrifying *Charlie Hebdo* massacre; or in Denmark, home of *Jyllands-Posten* and the illustrators whose work in the newspaper ignited the Cartoon Crisis of 2005–2006. Finally, there is the intrinsic danger that restrictions can be abused to hush the voices of legitimate democratic opposition.

People on both the right and the left have warned of a crisis of democracy, resulting from poor social cohesion in their societies. Individualisation, inequality and immigration have all been highlighted as factors that undermine national cohesion, which is emphasised as a key element of a well-functioning democracy.

In many places there are growing gaps in levels of participation and representation. The young and the disadvantaged are less involved in civil society and are more likely to be stay-at-home voters.

In parallel, the political parties, once mass movements with strong links to civil society, have become more elitist and more reliant on public funding and private donations. Since 1980, party membership in most Western European countries has shrunk 25–75%.

Too much partisanship in has also been flagged as a problem when it results in polarization, such as we have witnessed in the US. Here the ideological distance between Republicans and Democrats has grown, political positions have become more unidimensional, and mutual recognition has to large degree been replaced with spite and moralization. A polarized political climate undermines the opportunities for compromise and misleads many voters to prioritize own policy preferences over respect for democratic principles - thus creating a fertile ground for undemocratic initiatives.

Voter turnout in old, established democracies has generally declined since the 1970s, from 75% to 65%, although numbers vary greatly. The steepest drops have been seen in the United States, France, Switzerland and Japan, where only 40–60% of eligible voters make their voice heard. A few countries still have a good turnout, including Denmark, where parliamentary elections usually attract at least 85% of voters.

International affairs also have a variety of pessimists up in arms. Self-conscious autocracies, notably China and Russia, refuse democracy at home and seek to undermine it abroad, while the US has toned down its focus on democracy in foreign relations.

Some malign the European Union as an elitist project that lacks democratic legitimacy: The European Commission is not an elected body, yet it has the right to propose new legislation. Others point out that although the members of the European Parliament are directly elected, voter turnout is abysmal – and indeed, the average turnout for the 2019 European Parliament election was 51%. The Slovakians took the 'stay-at-home voter prize' with just 23% bothering to drop by the ballot box.

What is more, populist parties have increased their electoral support in many countries. Their anti-elitist agendas and claims to be the extended arm of 'common people' can be translated into anti-pluralist policies and undue power concentration.

Finally, pessimists often argue that *more* globalisation means *less* democracy, as it becomes harder for ordinary citizens to hold politicians accountable – since it is harder to see whether certain changes result from global developments or national policies. In addition, globalisation dictates certain policies for countries that want to remain on good terms with global financial markets and corporations. As the impact of national decision-making shrinks, they say, financial inequality in and among nations rises, making it ever harder for the disempowered to make their voices heard.

NO APOCALYPSE NOW

Fortunately, there are many indications that those who predict democracy's doom are jumping the gun. Despite terrorist attacks, decreasing voter turnout and party membership, and the rise of globalisation, the world has never been as democratic as it has in the past decade.

What is more, in many places around the world, women and religious, ethnic and sexual minorities have more political influence today than before, and politically active citizens have more ways than ever of finding and sharing information. This enables new types of involvement, and also more control and critical monitoring of those entrusted with political power.

It may sound surprising, but the EU is actually quite democratic compared to other international organisations. In fact, the mutual obligations of EU cooperation have been an important factor in ensuring both economic development and democratic progress and stability throughout Europe.

When it comes to the sometimes volatile liquid of democracy, the question of whether we ought to regard the proverbial glass as half empty or half full is one that each of us must decide for ourselves. On one hand, we must be wary of making every little molehill into a mountain. On the other, it is incontestable that the democracies of this world are neither flawless nor fit to solve every problem we have. Nevertheless, seen over time, the method of government of the people and by the people is plainly best *for* the people, as it generally delivers more life, liberty and happiness than the alternatives.

Winston Churchill, the British prime minister during World War II, neatly summed this up when he referred to democracy as "the worst form of Government except for all those other forms that have been tried from time to time". I agree, and since we have no better alternative, our most prudent course of action is to constantly and consistently uphold and defend democracy whenever we find it threatened.